HAL•LEONARD INSTRUMENTAL PLAY-ALONG

TENOR SAX

AUDIO ACCESS INCLUDED

PLAYBACK+
Speed • Pitch • Balance • Loop

STAR WARS™

MUSIC FROM ALL NINE FILMS

Audio arrangements by Peter Deneff

To access audio, visit:
www.halleonard.com/mylibrary

"Enter Code"
6413-1811-7719-9623

ISBN 978-1-70510-712-6

HAL•LEONARD®

Visit Hal Leonard Online at
www.halleonard.com

Contact us:
Hal Leonard
7777 West Bluemound Road
Milwaukee, WI 53213
Email: info@halleonard.com

In Europe, contact:
Hal Leonard Europe Limited
42 Wigmore Street
Marylebone, London, W1U 2RN
Email: info@halleonardeurope.com

In Australia, contact:
Hal Leonard Australia Pty. Ltd.
4 Lentara Court
Cheltenham, Victoria, 3192 Australia
Email: info@halleonard.com.au

ACROSS THE STARS

(Love Theme from *"STAR WARS: ATTACK OF THE CLONES"*)

TENOR SAX

Music by JOHN WILLIAMS

AHCH-TO ISLAND
from *STAR WARS: THE LAST JEDI*

TENOR SAX

Music by JOHN WILLIAMS

BATTLE OF THE HEROES

from *STAR WARS: REVENGE OF THE SITH*

TENOR SAX

By JOHN WILLIAMS

ff

CANTINA BAND

from *STAR WARS: A NEW HOPE*

TENOR SAX

Music by JOHN WILLIAMS

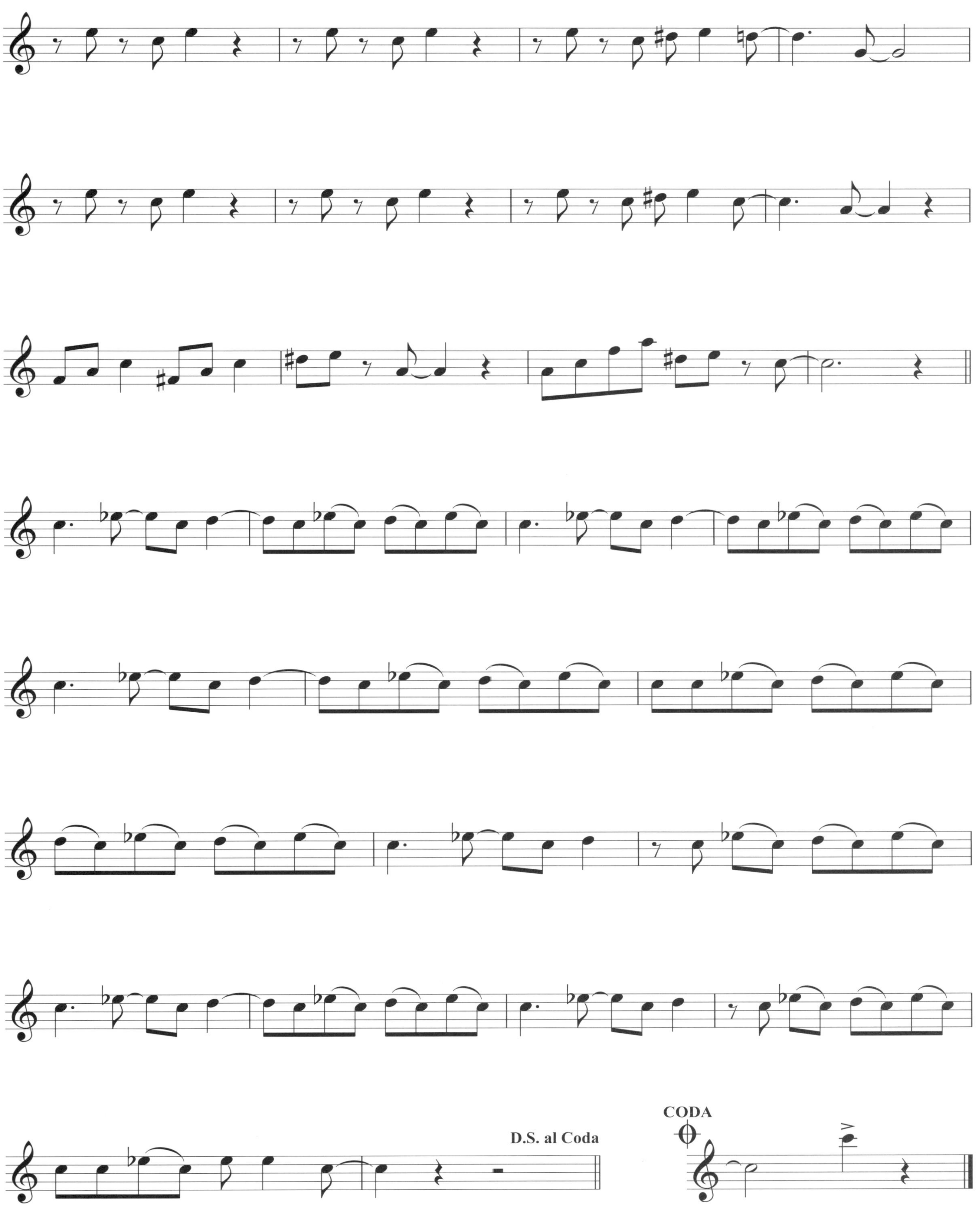
D.S. al Coda
CODA

DUEL OF THE FATES

from *STAR WARS: THE PHANTOM MENACE*

TENOR SAX

Music by JOHN WILLIAMS

4
f
6
mp
mf
f
3
3
ff

THE FOREST BATTLE

from *STAR WARS: RETURN OF THE JEDI*

TENOR SAX

Music by JOHN WILLIAMS

2
2
mf
4
4
f
mf

HAN SOLO AND THE PRINCESS

from *STAR WARS: THE EMPIRE STRIKES BACK*

TENOR SAX

Music by JOHN WILLIAMS

THE IMPERIAL MARCH

(Darth Vader's Theme)

from *STAR WARS: THE EMPIRE STRIKES BACK*

TENOR SAX

Music by JOHN WILLIAMS

MARCH OF THE RESISTANCE

from *STAR WARS: THE FORCE AWAKENS*

TENOR SAX

Music by JOHN WILLIAMS

3
mf
mp
mf
f
f
ff
fff

MAY THE FORCE BE WITH YOU

from *STAR WARS: A NEW HOPE*

TENOR SAX

Music by JOHN WILLIAMS

THE RISE OF SKYWALKER

from *STAR WARS: THE RISE OF SKYWALKER*

TENOR SAX

Composed by JOHN WILLIAMS

PRINCESS LEIA'S THEME

from *STAR WARS: A NEW HOPE*

TENOR SAX

Music by JOHN WILLIAMS

rit.

REY'S THEME

from *STAR WARS: THE FORCE AWAKENS*

TENOR SAX

Music by JOHN WILLIAMS

mf
Broadly
f
ff
rit.
Tempo I
mp
p
rit.
pp

STAR WARS
(Main Theme)
from *STAR WARS: A NEW HOPE*

TENOR SAX

Music by JOHN WILLIAMS

THRONE ROOM *and* END TITLE

from *STAR WARS: A NEW HOPE*

TENOR SAX

Music by JOHN WILLIAMS

YODA'S THEME

from *STAR WARS: THE EMPIRE STRIKES BACK*

TENOR SAX

Music by JOHN WILLIAMS